LEADERSHIP

How to Be a Leader, Boost Your Business Skills and Influence People

ZACHARY D. WEST

Introduction

I want to thank you and congratulate you for buying the book, *"Leadership"*.

This book contains proven steps and strategies on how to develop leadership skills.

What does it take to be a leader? A lot of people are thrown into leadership positions without knowing the answer to this question. An employee who is suddenly promoted to a managerial position may ask this question. An introverted business owner, for example, may also think about what it takes for him to become a good leader when trying to rally his employees to work harder. Their ability to answer this question and apply the answer in their own situation will be the basis of their success.

We all need to become leaders at some point in our lives. It is important that all of us try to answer this question on our own ways. You will find most of the answers you need in this book. Just like any other aspect of self-improvement, leadership starts with improving yourself. Once you have gained confidence and competence in your leadership skills, the next step is to use management and social strategies to influence other people. If you apply the suggestions in this book, you will learn what it takes to become a leader. You can then apply that knowledge into your own life and career.

Thanks again for buying this book, I hope you enjoy it!

A leader is like a shepherd: he stays behind the flock, letting the most nimble go on ahead, whereupon the others follow, not realizing that all along they are being directed from behind.

- Nelson Mandela

Chapter 1 – What is Leadership?

Leadership is not just a skill. It is made up of a combination of social and management skills. It is the ability to push a group to achieve goals that they normally cannot achieve without a leader's guidance. History is filled with stories of great men and women who rallied groups of people into doing nearly impossible feats. A common theme among these stories is that the leader was able to unite people to work together for a common goal.

Leaders have influence over other people. They use this influence to push people into working together. Without leadership, people will work separately to pursue their own goals. A leader shows these people that they can achieve their goals faster if they work with the group.

Position is not leadership

You should not take a person's position as a sign that he or she is a good leader. True leaders do not need a title to do their job. They take leadership responsibilities even if they are not required to by their organization. They know that their skills can help the people around them and use these when needed.

Start developing leadership early

Start developing your leadership skills even when you are not yet in the position to lead. This is the best time to learn because there will be no pressure on you to get things done. If you succeed, however, people will start to notice that you have excellent leadership skills. If you are an employee, this will increase your chances of getting a promotion. If you manage your own business, your leadership skills will attract the best

1

workers to work for you.

The two important qualities that will distinguish you as a leader

From this point on, you need to think that you are being observed. You need to consider all challenges as tests. If you do well in these tests, people will notice it and they will start to rely on your leadership skills.

To survive these tests, you need to have the following qualities:

1. Positive Observable Characteristics

Before you can influence people, you first need to gain their trust. You can only gain their trust if you consistently show qualities that have positive effects on the group. First, you need to create a positive impression based on the way you look. After that, you need to copy some of the positive characteristics of the leaders you admire. The best way to learn about leadership is by mimicking the positive characteristics of successful leaders.

Secondly, you should also learn about the people who you want to lead so that you will know that qualities they look for in a leader. You may learn about their language and their culture to understand them better.

Thirdly, you also need to show that you have the intellectual and social skills needed to lead. Show that you follow ethical standards of the industry and that you are a trustworthy person. If you have this kind of reputation, people will begin to trust you.

2. Being An Achiever

If you do all the things suggested above, it will be easier for you to gain the trust of your followers. However, the true test of your leadership skills comes when there are expectations for you to reach goals. Anyone can become likable when there is no pressure, but only those with refined leadership skills can act objectively when there is pressure to get things done.

To make the foundation of your leadership status strong, you need to shine in these opportunities. You can do this by managing people, emotions and available resources to reach the goal of the group.

Chapter 2 – Hierarchy of Leadership

There are different levels of leadership based on the number of people one leads. You start with the first stage:

Stage 1: Being a Follower

In the beginning, no one considers you a leader. You are following another leader, just like everybody else. This is where you begin to develop your skills.

In this stage, you learn how to analyze people and how to influence them based on your analysis. You also learn about how the group works in this stage. Most people do not actively learn how their social environment works. To learn, you need to observe the people around you. To become an excellent leader, you need to have the skill of reading the motivation behind people's actions. If you know what motivates the people who surround, you can easily influence them into working together.

Stage 2: Leading Small Groups

In this stage, you begin to use your knowledge and apply it to develop your leadership skills. You try out different strategies for influencing people. You retain the skills and strategies that work and learn from those that do not.

You test these strategies while leading smaller groups. Early in your career, your goal is to gain experience in your field. The people around you will never look at you as a leader until you have the track record to prove your competence.

You will need a series of successful projects before people will begin to notice you. Once they do, you may be promoted to higher positions.

Stage 3: Being an Organizational Leader

In this stage, people around you have begun to realize that you have excellent leadership skills. You may already be in a leadership position in your group. You may also be given larger projects with more people involved.

Organizational leaders have more weight on their shoulders. However, business leaders in this group are rewarded well for their success. This is the stage where most people spend the majority of their lives. If you are an employee, this is the stage where you climb the corporate ladder. If you have your own business, this is the stage where your business grows under your leadership.

In the early parts of being an organizational leader, only a few people know about your leadership skills. You only have influence over people that you have worked with in the past. If you have a choice, you may want to bring some of these people with you in your new projects.

You can gain more attention as you are promoted to higher positions. The people who hear of your rise may ask around about you. Through word-of-mouth, your reputation will become known throughout your organization.

As this happens, you can influence more people. However, with more attention on you, your actions will be greatly scrutinized by the people in your organization. Successes will widen your reputation as a leader. However, just one misstep may undo all the positive results and fruits of your hard work. In the words of one of the most recognized leaders in business, Warren Buffett: "It takes twenty years to build a reputation, and five minutes to ruin it. If you think about that, you'll do things differently".

Stage 4: Being an Industry Leader

After years of hard work, success and failure, you may become considered as an industry leader. Industry leaders never stop learning. They never become satisfied with their skills. They start projects that affect not only their own companies, but also the whole industry. Some of them are even admired by people outside of their industries.

You will only reach this stage if you never give up on learning and reaching higher goals. Even people outside of your company will notice your leadership skills. People will look up to you because of your consistency in working hard and in reaching goals. When you are in this stage, people will listen to your every word.

Warren Buffett is an example of an industry leader. He has displayed his competence in investing money. When he talks about investing, everyone stops what he or she is doing and listens.

You may think that he was born with his leadership skills. He was not. He started out just like you and me. Over the years, he proved his value in his company and his industry. He never stopped learning. Most people his age have already retired. At 85 years old, he is still at the helm of his investing company.

Zachary D. West

Chapter 3 – Start by Improving Yourself

If you want to be an effective business leader and climb the hierarchy of leadership discussed in the previous chapter, you need to start by improving yourself. Here are the characteristics that you need to work on:

1. Developing the right skills in your job

Start by obtaining all the skills that your job requires. Your aim is to become an expert in your chosen industry. You need to learn the fundamental skills in your field. As you master the fundamentals, you can start learning more advanced skills and knowledge.

Great leaders are not good at everything. However, their followers acknowledge that they are good at something. Warren buffet, for example, is a leader in the field of investing. He acknowledges that he is not a master in all types of investments. If he encounters a new type of investment, he needs to study it first to be able to make the right investing decision. In his own words, he stays within his "circle of competence", which he has spent decades developing.

Instead of mastering all investment skills, Warren Buffet emphasizes focusing on this circle of competence. This is an area of knowledge in which you are an expert. As you learn more about your field through formal study and first-hand experience, you can easily widen your circle of competence.

2. Communicating like a leader

Great leaders are excellent communicators. All your ideas will not matter if you do not know how to communicate them effectively to your followers. There are many types of communication that a leader needs to master.

First, you need to develop the ability to talk to a huge crowd. Most people are afraid of talking to large groups of people. If you develop this skill, you will have an advantage over your competition in leadership positions. Here is a process that you can follow on how to talk to big groups:

a.   Identify your objective for talking to the group

Always have an objective when you talk to a group. When you gather people to listen to you, you are using up their valuable time. Without a clearly stated objective, the meeting will have no direction. People may waste time talking about irrelevant topics.

b.   Create a message that accomplishes your objectives

If you are not used to communicating with groups of people, you need to prepare your message in advance so that you can practice it before delivering it to your target audience. This will increase your chances of delivering an authoritative message.

c.   Write down your message and practice it in front of a mirror

Saying your message in front of the mirror helps you practice your gestures, facial expressions and other non-verbal cues. Beginners often neglect these small details, but they are just as important as your voice.

d.   Practice it in front of people you trust

For the most important messages, you need to practice in front of a smaller audience before delivering it to the big crowd. This allows you to become accustomed to speaking aloud in front of a group of people. You can adjust your actions based on their tips.

Practicing in front of a smaller group also allows you to test the effectiveness of your message in terms of accomplishing your intended objectives. Your listeners may be able to give you recommendations on how you can improve your message.

e.   Refine your message according to their feedback

Before delivering your message, you need to refine it based on what you learn from your practice. You need to refine not only the content, but also the manner through which you will deliver it. You need to give attention to your voice, as well as your non-verbal cues.

f.   Deliver your practiced message to its intended audience

If you are satisfied with your message, it is time to deliver it to its intended audience. You will not become a master orator on your first try. However, based on the effectiveness of your message, you can achieve your objectives.

Take every opportunity to talk in front of a group. If you practice this skill often, you can get rid of your fear of talking to a crowd. You can do it as naturally as talking to one person.

3. Learning to read people

As a leader, you should constantly observe the people you lead. You do this to know what motivates and demotivates them. When you see people in your organization who are working hard, for example, try to understand what motivates them. Observe as carefully when they are not motivated, and try to identify the reasons.

There are also times when asking people directly about their motivations may not be the best method. You may need to do your own investigation to find out the reasons behind their actions. This way, your followers will not know that you are keeping tabs on the factors that motivate them to work. Knowing what makes people work harder will allow you to boost their performance when there is a need for it.

4. Learning to Delegate

Next, learn to delegate important tasks to other people. As a leader, your time and energy are more important than those of other members. Make sure that you only spend them on the most important tasks.

It is advisable to delegate tasks that other members of your group can do effectively. When you delegate, you need to use the following guidelines:

a. Make sure that the person you delegate to has the skills to get the job done.

b. Make sure that he or she is given enough time and resources to do the task.

c. Avoid micromanaging their tasks. Allow the team member to work on the task independently.

d. Make the objectives of the task clear before letting them start

5. Learning to Network

An effective leader has useful relationships in his industry. If you want to improve your ability as a leader, you need to start developing relationships with influential people.

There are times when your team's problems can only be solved with the help of people from the outside. You need to have relationships with those who may become helpful to your team or company.

Building these connections should be done actively. As you become better known as a leader, you will come to know other leaders in your industry. You may meet them by chance, as you do business or they may purposely seek you out.

To hasten the networking process, you need to identify people who may become helpful in the future. Start developing relationships with them by offering your help when they need it. This way, they may also return the favor when you and your team are the ones in need.

Chapter 4 – Building Trust Inside and Outside of your Organization

Trust makes up the foundation of your image as a leader. Improve your reputation and make sure to show your trustworthiness to both your followers and your superiors. If your superiors believe that they can trust you, they are more likely to put you in leadership positions. They will base their decision on your reputation. When you first meet your followers, they will also judge you based on your reputation. If your reputation is that of a dishonest person, no one will believe that you have what it takes to be a leader.

Here are the factors that you need to consider when developing a trustworthy reputation:

1. Become aware of the idea you represent

Great leaders represent an idea, from which their charisma is derived. President Barrack Obama, for example, represented the idea of change in his journey to becoming president. The American people wanted change from the previous administrations at the time. Winston Churchill represented toughness and resilience to the British people. These were the qualities that the Brits needed from their leader when they were repeatedly bombed by the Nazis.

You need to think of the idea that you represent to the people you lead. Embody that idea in your appearance, messages, in the way you speak and even in your actions. If people see consistency in the idea you represent, your appearance and your actions, they are more likely to trust you.

Business people often become the face of the business they own. Richard Branson, the founder of the Virgin Group, has been the face of business for more than three decades. The image of his company is based on his personal image – that of fun.

If you become successful as a leader, your image, your reputation and the idea that you represent rub off on the organizations that you lead. It is important to protect your image at all costs. Even when you are just starting out, you need to keep your record clean. Any mistake that goes against your image may be used against you by your competition to destroy your reputation.

2. Believe in your organization and your cause

The leaders of big companies have genuine belief in the organization they represent. If you do not trust the company that you work for and if you do not believe in its vision, influencing others to work hard for that organization will be difficult for you.

If you currently do not have a strong belief in the organization that you represent, you need to start learning about it. Start learning about how the organization's products or services help the public. Learn its mission and the strategies it uses to achieve it. Learn about the leaders who run your organization. Check their interviews online. By hearing them speak about your organization, you will know why they are passionate about it. You will also learn about their projections for the future of the organization. Another great thing about this is that you can learn lessons about leadership from them. As you observe them, you may learn their leadership style and you may apply what you learn to the people you lead.

Once you learn about the value of the organization to the general public, you will have a greater reason to trust it and believe in its mission. To show your followers that you believe in the organization, you need to exhibit enthusiasm in the way you work and communicate. Explain to the people that you work with why your jobs are important. When your organization is being attacked, you should defend it.

Another way to show that you believe in the organization that you represent is by showing loyalty. When you are loyal to your organization, this shows your followers that the organization has treated you well for all your hard work. You will know whether your loyalty will be rewarded by observing other people who have been loyal to your company. These are the people who have spent their lives working there.

3. Find ways to improve the team's ability to reach its goals

Now that you know the goals of your organization, you need to contribute to the realization of these goals by sharing your own ideas on how the group can do that. You can climb the leadership ladder faster if you have suggestions on how the group can perform better in reaching its goals.

You do not have to come up with these ideas yourself. You can research about how other organizations and companies reach similar goals. You can then refine their methods and apply these to your own group. After coming up with ways on how to improve your group's performance, you should create a plan on how you can implement your ideas.

Keep learning about your own industry so that you will always have fresh ideas to try. Great leaders think of themselves as students of the industry they are in. They do not fear innovations. Instead of maintaining the status quo, they try to find areas where they can innovate to reach the intended goals faster.

4. Show consistent competence

Now that you have shown that you believe in the organization that you work for, the next step is to become consistently competent in helping the organization reach its goals. Competence is one of the most important qualities of a leader. Your followers will only follow you if they see that you have the skills to lead them in the right direction.

They will judge you based on how you act during crucial moments in the process of accomplishing your tasks. They will also judge you based on how you act in stressful situations. Among the members of a company, the people who can get tasks done regularly and who are immune to pressure are the first to be considered for leadership positions.

5. Assume leadership responsibilities

Do not wait for your organization to give you a leadership position before taking leadership responsibilities. Once you have the confidence to lead, you should start influencing the people that you work with.

Every time you notice that there is a need for someone to take the leadership position, you need to step up to the task. You should be constantly looking for these opportunities. You can find such opportunities when the group you are working with is given a goal and no leader is clearly assigned. Sometimes, you need to step up even when there is an assigned leader. It is common for people with inadequate leadership skills to be given leadership positions. If such a person is assigned as the leader of your group, they may show areas of incompetence early on. They may run away from their leadership responsibilities when the group needs them the most.

When such leadership problem arises, you need to look for ways to help the group. This is what a true leader will do. If the assigned leader is not present during crucial parts of a project, for example, you should make your superiors aware of it and ask them if you can take the leadership position to complete the project.

There may also be times when the assigned leader shows difficulties managing people's motivation. This often happens when there is a communication gap between the leader and their followers. If this is the case, you need to take the responsibility of motivating them. Ask the assigned group leader if you can try to talk to the group.

By taking leadership responsibilities, you will be noticed by your superiors and you will be one of the first people that they will consider when they are looking for someone to fill the position of a leader. This also gives you an opportunity to practice your skills without the pressure of being in the leadership position.

6. Influence the people around you to work harder

Even when there are no immediate goals to be completed, you should still look for leadership opportunities that you can fill. One way to do this is by influencing the people around you to work harder. To do this, you need to know the people that you work with. Most leaders make the mistake of putting a wall between them and the people they work with. They expect their underlings to follow their orders without question. They do not consider the human factor of management.

You need to avoid this behavior. When you separate yourself from the people you lead, you become indifferent of the challenges they face. As a business leader, you must be the communication bridge between the people you lead and the organization you represent. Most companies prioritize the bottom line of their business. They will pressure their workers to work hard without considering the experiences they are going through. To become an effective leader, you need to know your people, so you will know exactly how you can motivate them to work even harder.

Chapter 5 - Strengthening your Image as a Leader

Using the tips in the previous chapter, you can gain the trust of your followers. The next step is to keep working to strengthen your image as a leader.

To do this, you need to show the following qualities:

1. Confidence

So far, this book has given you tips on how you can improve as an individual and as a leader. These improvements are meant to bring you private and public successes. As you succeed in various areas of life, you will begin to become confident in your job, your business and your leadership skills.

Aside from your own skills, you should also show confidence in the people you lead and the organization or company you represent. You can show this in your speech and in your actions. To show that you trust the people you lead, for example, you should delegate some of the tasks to them.

Once you've developed your confidence, you need to protect it at all costs. The best way to protect your confidence is to keep a solution-focused mindset. People who lack confidence in themselves and the people around them tend to blame others when problems arise.

To show that you are confident in the face of challenges, you should directly look for the solution to the problem as soon as you hear about it. You no longer waste time on blaming others for the problem. By doing this, you show your followers that you are confident about your team's ability to solve the problem.

I have written an entire book on the topic of confidence and self-esteem. Like this book, it contains time-tested strategies and tools to help you become confident, in any situation. If you want to learn more, you may look up the book on Amazon <u>Confidence: How To Boost Your Self Confidence and Self Esteem, Turn Your Life Around And Be Confident In Any Situation.</u>

2. A constant positive attitude

Having a solution-focused mindset also creates a constant positive attitude. You will need this kind of attitude especially when trying to accomplish long and difficult tasks.

When a leader displays a bad attitude, it also affects the attitude of the people they leads. It affects their work ethic and their motivation. Show that you have a positive attitude towards the people whom you work with. You can do this by adapting your mood when you communicate with your followers. People with positive attitude never react with rage. They wait for their negative mood to subside before they communicate with their followers. Another tip is to smile before you speak. Both in person and on the phone, this simple trick does wonder at communicating a positive attitude.

Keeping a positive attitude keeps your team motivated and upbeat when working towards the team's objectives. If they are in a good mood, they will be more motivated to work.

3. Trust in the team's creativity

As mentioned earlier in the book, you need to keep learning so that you will always have something new to teach your team. This attitude will be useful when the problems you face as a leader require ingenuity. When solving these types of problems, you can strengthen your image as a leader by considering the ideas of other people. This shows that you trust the people you lead to solve the problem. By doing this, you minimize the team's reliance on you to get the things done. You encourage each member to think of solutions to the challenges that the entire team faces.

If your team is accustomed to solving problems on their own, they will have the initiative to solve future problems on their own. They may let you know about these problems only when they have already solved it.

4. Commitment to the team and the goal

You can also strengthen your image as a leader by showing commitment to your followers and the goals that you are trying to reach. You can show commitment in the consistency of your actions. When you become a leader in your field, you will influence others to take the same path you did. Members of the younger generation who look up to you may choose to take the same job or apply to the same company.

They will do this because you have shown commitment in the field, company and the people that you work with. If you give up your commitment on any of these, the people who follow you may also give up on the path they have taken. As a leader, you have the power to influence others. You influence them not only in your good examples, but also in your bad behaviors.

Your lack of commitment will also affect the members of your team. If you show lack of enthusiasm in your work, your team may interpret this as a sign that you are not committed to reaching the goal. This will also affect their own enthusiasm towards the team's goals.

5. Willingness to take calculated risks

There are times when you need to trust your intuition in making leadership decisions. Though you should try to be objective in your decision-making, you should show no fear when you need to take risks. This is an important quality of a business leader. Leaders who are afraid to take risks tend to limit the growth of the organization they lead.

Even if you are not afraid of taking risks, you need to consider all the rewards and benefits of all the options. Only take risks when the reward of being right justifies the decision. Practice taking calculated risks throughout your leadership career so that you will be ready to use this skill when the stakes are higher. As Tony Robbins argues, the best way to make better decisions is to make more of them.

Conclusion

Thank you again for buying this book!

I hope this book was able to help you to find out what it takes to be a leader.

Apply the tips and strategies that you learned in this book in your own career. You should then seek out leadership opportunities in your job. Use these opportunities to practice your leadership skills. As you continue to learn about human nature and gain more experience, you will surely improve your ability to lead small and large groups.

Finally, if you enjoyed this book, then I'd like to ask you for a favor, would you be kind enough to leave a review for this book on Amazon? It'd be greatly appreciated!

Thank you and good luck!

Preview Of 'Wealth: Accumulating Money, Building Wealth And Staying Rich Through Sound Financial Management And Time-Tested Strategies"

While only a few people will admit this, earning enough money is crucial in this time and age. While money does not guarantee happiness or even a good life, it does help to make life better. It helps you (and your loved ones) get your needs adequately and get more and better life opportunities. The problem is that a lot of people don't know how to earn money the right way. You have to earn money the right way to ensure that you'll have more than enough in the bank as you ride into the sunset. Here are some tips to live by to earn money and build wealth.

1.   Find a niche

Regardless of what money-making methods you use, it is important to find your niche. After all, if you don't fit in, there's no way you can prosper there (and in effect rack up the cash at a high rate). There are multiple considerations to take when you're finding a niche. First, it has to fit in your interests. If you like what you're doing, learning and taking action becomes much easier.

Second, you've got to have the skills for it. If you have the knack for a particular field, you're more likely than not to achieve success. Third, it has to be rewarding. If it does not provide you either progress or satisfaction, it's probably not the right field for you. Not all people find their niche, but those who do will, more likely than not, end up successful.

2....

Head to Amazon.com to find out more!

Zachary D. West

Check Out My Other Books

Below you'll find some of my other books that are popular on Amazon and Kindle as well. Simply look them out on Amazon. check them out. Alternatively, you can visit my author page on Amazon to see other work done by me.

Wealth: Accumulating Money, Building Wealth and Staying Rich Through Sound Financial Management And Time-Tested Strategies.

Confidence: How To Boost Your Self Confidence and Self Esteem, Turn Your Life Around And Be Confident In Any Situation

Positive Thinking: How to Change Your Negative Mindset on Life, Build the Habit of Positive Thoughts and Live a Happy and Successful Life.

You can find them on Amazon.com by searching for my author name. Thank you!

www.ingramcontent.com/pod-product-compliance
Lightning Source LLC
Chambersburg PA
CBHW071836200526
45169CB00019B/1577